RUTH AMOS

BOOTS THAT FIT

A COMPANION WORKBOOK

How to serve God and your community in a way that suits your unique gifts and personality.

ISBN: 9780648291398
Copyright © 2024 Ruth Amos
Cover design, typesetting and illustrations by Meng Koach

I feel that many of us could do with a few pointers about how we can find the thing God wants us to do with our lives. How we can build our identity on him and how we can serve others in a way that is uniquely ours. How we can figure out when and why and how to say 'No' to even just a few of the many, many requests that come our way each day. And how we can do that with peace and without feeling crushing guilt.

As we move through the seasons of life, each of us can have a time where we wonder, 'who am I?' It can happen when we leave school, or when we get married (or don't get married though we want to), or when our children become more independent and don't need us as much, or when we retire from a fulfilling career and now don't know what to do with each day.

I'm not pretending that I'll be able to solve all of your problems, but I have learned a few things in my own struggles to find boots that fit. In this book, I'd like to share with you what I've learned about finding a way to serve that is congruent with your personality and temperament, your values and your energy levels. About finding your identity and doing what is yours to do.

This workbook is designed to be a companion to *Boots That Fit* by Ruth Amos. While this book contains a small introduction to each of the activities, my thoughts, heart and teaching on these important topics are all described much more fully in *Boots That Fit*, available in print and as an ebook at all online retailers and at **ruthamos.com.au**.

PART 1

WHO

PERSONALITY TYPES

"Know thyself."
– Delphic maxim

"There are two kinds of people in the world: those who divide the world into two kinds of people, and those who don't."
– Gretchen Rubin

One of the things I have found helpful when thinking about who I am, is just to analyse my own behaviour. Try answering these questions:

✎ What kinds of activities or work do you enjoy?

_____

_____

_____

_____

_____

_____

_____

_____

✎ How do you actually spend your time? (For example, you might think you enjoy a particular activity such as paddle boarding, but if you never get around to it, and instead you get out the bike and go for a ride every Saturday morning, then that shows you that you possibly find riding more enjoyable than paddle boarding.)

_____

_____

_____

_____

_____

✎ What's an activity or task that you would do as a regular thing, even if you didn't get paid?

_____

_____

_____

_____

_____

_____

_____

_____

_____

_____

Are there themes in your answers to these questions? Are the activities inside or outside activities? Are they with people or would you do them alone? Do they involve organising and sorting things out or would you be making a larger mess when you do them? Are they more practical activities where you work with your hands or are they more cerebral and require you to think academically?

VALUES

"It's not hard to make decisions when you know what your values are."
– Roy E. Disney

"Values are like fingerprints. Nobody's are the same. But you leave 'em all over everything you do."
– Elvis Presley

Values define what is important to you. Your values guide your behaviours and decisions. They are attributes of the person you want to be. When you live according to your values you live with authenticity and personal integrity.

Use the following values list to define your top three to five values. (You can also download a list from **ruthamos.com.au/worksheets/**).

1. Cut the list up so that each value statement is on a separate piece of paper.

2. Divide the values into three piles:
   1) I really value this;
   2) I sort of value this; and
   3) I don't value this at all.

3. Get rid of piles 2 and 3 and continue to sort through Pile 1 until you have your three to five most important values.

Abundance	Commonality	Ethics
Acceptance	Communication	Excellence
Accomplishment	Community	Excitement
Accountability	Compassion	Experience
Accuracy	Competence	Exploration
Achievement	Concentration	Expressiveness
Adaptability	Confidence	Facilitation
Advancement	Connection	Fairness
Adventure	Consciousness	Faith
Affection	Consistency	Fame
Alertness	Contentment	Family
Altruism	Contribution	Fame
Ambition	Control	Fearlessness
Amusement	Conviction	Ferociousness
Appreciation	Cooperation	Fidelity
Assertiveness	Courage	Finances
Attentiveness	Courtesy	Finesse
Authenticity	Creation	Fitness
Authority	Creativity	Focus
Autonomy	Credibility	Foresight
Awareness	Curiosity	Forgiveness
Balance	Curiosity	Fortitude
Beauty	Decisiveness	Freedom
Boldness	Dedication	Friendship
Bravery	Dependability	Fun
Brilliance	Determination	Generosity
Calm	Development	Genius
Candor	Devotion	Giving People a Chance
Capable	Dignity	Goodness
Career	Discipline	Grace
Carefulness	Discovery	Gratitude
Caring	Diversity	Greatness
Certainty	Drive	Growth
Challenge	Effectiveness	Happiness
Change	Efficiency	Hard work
Charisma	Empathy	Harmony
Charity	Empowerment	Health
Citizenship	Encouragement	Home
Clarity	Endurance	Honesty
Cleanliness	Energy	Honor
Clear	Enjoyment	Hope
Cleverness	Entertainment	Humanity
Comfort	Enthusiasm	Humility
Commitment	Entrepreneurship	Humor
Common sense	Equality	Imagination

Improvement	Playfulness	Solitude
Independence	Pleasure	Speed
Individuality	Poise	Spirit
Influence	Popularity	Spirituality
Inner Harmony	Potential	Spontaneity
Innovation	Power	Stability
Inquisitiveness	Presence	Status
Insight	Pride in Your Work	Stewardship
Inspiration	Productivity	Strength
Integrity	Professionalism	Structure
Intelligence	Prosperity	Success
Intensity	Purpose	Support
Intuitive	Quality	Surprise
Invention	Realism	Sustainability
Involvement	Reason	Talent
Joy	Reciprocity	Teamwork
Justice	Recognition	Temperance
Kindness	Recreation	Thankfulness
Knowledge	Reflection	Thoroughness
Lawful	Relationship	Thoughtfulness
Leadership	Religion	Timeliness
Learning	Renewal	Tolerance
Liberty	Reputation	Toughness
Logic	Respect	Tradition
Love	Responsibility	Tranquility
Loyalty	Restraint	Transparency
Mastery	Results	Trust
Maturity	Reverence	Trustworthiness
Meaning	Rigor	Truth
Meaningful Work	Risk	Understanding
Moderation	Satisfaction	Uniqueness
Motivation	Security	Unity
Openness	Self-reliance	Valor
Optimism	Selflessness	Victory
Order	Sensitivity	Vigor
Organization	Serenity	Vision
Originality	Service	Vitality
Passion	Significance	Wealth
Patience	Silence	Wellness
Peace	Simplicity	Willingness
Performance	Sincerity	Winning
Persistence	Skillfulness	Wisdom
Personal Development		Wonder

☑ Choosing one of your most important values, write a paragraph, draw a picture or make a collage or mood board about how you express this value in your everyday life.

☑ If you're facing a difficult situation or a major decision, write a paragraph, draw a picture or make a collage or mood board showing how these values could guide you or support you in it.

YOUR LIFE NOW

"Life is what happens while you are busy making other plans."
– John Lennon

"What a wonderful life I've had! I only wish I'd realised it sooner."
– Sidonie Gabrielle Colette

When we're very busy we can just keep going and going, without really thinking about what we're doing. We're working hard, but perhaps we're working on the wrong things. We're making progress, but perhaps in the wrong direction. Things that are our priorities can be squashed into the background of our lives, receiving ten minutes every fortnight, and things that we don't really care so much about can somehow grow to take up hours of each week, just by accident.

I'd like you to make time to sit down and really think about what your life is like now. To think about where you are, so that you can then think about where you'd like to be. I encourage you to take a little time to think about how you are spending your days, how you are spending the time you have available to you. What are you filling your life with? Is that what you want? Does something need to change?

✎ Make a mind map of your life. Put yourself in the centre, and all the parts that make up your life around the outside. Make it as pretty or as plain as you like – this is your life!

MY LIFE
MIND MAP

Use the time tracker sheet (opposite page) to keep a record of your days. Fill the segments out as close to the activity as is possible. Don't wait days and then think back. Fill out the half-hour sections as you go.

If you need more sheets you can find them at **ruthamos.com.au/worksheets/**

🖉 Colour code the sections of your mind map and transfer those colours to your time tracker. Are you spending the most time on things that you think should get the most attention? Are you losing time to distractions and clutter?

	MONDAY	TUESDAY	WEDNESDAY	THURSDAY	FRIDAY	SATURDAY	SUNDAY
8:00am							
8:30							
9:00							
9:30							
10:00							
10:30							
11:00							
11:30							
12:00pm							
12:30							
1:00							
1:30							
2:00							
2:30							
3:00							
3:30							
4:00							
4:30							
5:00							
5:30							
6:00							
6:30							
7:00							
7:30							
8:00							

NOT JUST A BRAIN

"I am not merely a soul and spirit; I am an embodied human being, and my body is the temple of the Holy Spirit."
– Ruth Haley Barton

"Being an adult is pretty easy. You just feel tired all the time and tell people how tired you are, and they tell you how tired they are."
– Aaron Gillies

Whatever we choose to do, we will use our bodies to do it. To make the best use of our lives, we need to look after ourselves, not just the spiritual, emotional and mental parts of our beings, but also our physical selves.

We need to make sure we're looking after the five pillars of health:

1. Exercise
2. Nutrition
3. Sleep
4. Social Connection
5. Time to Switch Off/Relax

Which pillar of your life is the healthiest, getting the attention it needs?

_____

_____

_____

_____

Which pillar of your life needs more attention?

_____

_____

_____

_____

What do you think is stopping you from giving it that attention?

_____

_____

_____

_____

_____

☑ In the book *Getting Things Done*, David Allen asks 'what is the next action?' Changing your physical activities can be a daunting task. Below, write three 'next actions' you can do to prioritise looking after your physical self.

1.

2.

3.

☑ Make a date with a good friend to go for a walk together in nature. This will tick the physical exercise and social interaction boxes, give you sunlight (hence vitamin D), get you out in nature and hopefully contribute to better sleep.

LIMITING BELIEFS

"Comparison is the thief of joy."
– Theodore Roosevelt

"Then you will know the truth, and the truth will set you free."
– Jesus, in John 8:32 (NIV)

W hat's your picture of success? Are you viewing yourself as a failure because you are trying to live someone else's life? I've heard of people being squeezed into their parents' view of success, or maybe a view held by a respected teacher, but as you can see from my story, I found it just as easy to push myself to meet an ideal that was wrong for me. In order for us to find our own mission, we also need to understand what success really means for us. We need to stop comparing ourselves to others and stop believing the lies that have been spoken over us in the past or that come from deep within us.

Affirmations are small phrases that we repeat to ourselves to help us remember the truth. They can be truths that are accurate now, and they can also be aspirational truths.

✎ What are some limiting beliefs you hold about yourself?

_____

_____

_____

_____

_____

_____

✎ What affirmations will you use to fight against them?

_____

_____

_____

_____

_____

_____

✏️ Write out each affirmation five times a day for the next week.

1.

2.

3.

4.

5.

1.

2.

3.

4.

5.

1.

2.

3.

4.

5.

1.

2.

3.

4.

5.

1.

2.

3.

4.

5.

1.

2.

3.

4.

5.

1.

2.

3.

4.

5.

Scripture Affirmations

Take delight in the Lord and he will give you the desires of your heart.
Psalm 37:4

Do not be afraid; you will not be put to shame.
Isaiah 54:4a

Therefore my heart is glad and my tongue rejoices; my body also will rest secure.
Psalm 16:9

He who began a good work in you will carry it on to completion.
Philippians 1:6

For we live by faith, not by sight.
2 Corinthians 5:7

You will keep in perfect peace those whose minds are steadfast
because they trust in you.
Isaiah 26:3

Let us not become weary in doing good, for at the proper time we
will reap a harvest if we do not give up.
Galatians 6:9

For we are God's handiwork, created in Christ Jesus to do good works, which
God prepared in advance for us to do.
Ephesians 2:10

And my God will meet all your needs according to the riches of
his glory in Christ Jesus.
Philippians 4:19

For when I am weak, then I am strong.
2 Corinthians 12:10b

SHOULD

"There is nothing so useless as doing efficiently that which should not be done at all."
– Peter Drucker

"Next time you feel a should coming at you, ask yourself if it really belongs to you!"
– Kelly Corbet

So, you've looked at your life through the lens of your personality, and you've aligned your activities to your values. But if you're anything like me, there are a whole lot of activities that you're still going to try to do, because you've put them into another category. These are activities you feel like you need to do, even though they don't really suit your personality, and they don't necessarily align with your values.

These are the *shoulds*.

Shoulds are usually worthy and worthwhile activities. For me, they are activities that are highly thought of by my parents or even my grandparents. They are never things I want to do, but things that I'm feeling external pressure to do or some sort of obligation.

✎ Write three activities that you are attempting this month because you think you *should*.

✎ Now rephrase the sentence. What is the actual reason you are planning this activity? Is this now something that you can eliminate from your tasks or change so that you are not so resentful?

SEASONS

"There is a time for everything, and a season for every activity under the heavens."
– Ecclesiastes 3:1 (NIV)

"Be aware of what season you are in and give yourself the grace to be there."
– Kristen Dalton

Sometimes in life, all the mind maps, dreaming, personality-type exploration, time management and everything else will not help. Sometimes you have all the right intentions, but the universe conspires against you and you're stuck in a situation where you can't follow your dreams and nothing you do will make a difference to that.

What season are you in? Is it long-term? Is it time for a short sprint? Is it an open-ended season? What do you need to adjust to help you get through the season? What can you rejoice in that belongs to this season? Is it time to make sacrifices and larger changes? Is there a small change you can make so that you're still following your mission, even with the challenges you are facing right now?

Write a letter to yourself, thinking of yourself with sober judgement. What advice would you give if you were talking to a loved friend in exactly your situation?

Dear Beloved Friend,

DOING WHAT YOU LOVE

"I originally thought they were all just better at pretending to like the things I hated. Later, I was confounded: why did they love meeting big groups of people and socialising for hours and throwing big birthday parties when I didn't? I thought that there was something deeply wrong with me."
– Jessica Pan

Thinking about what you enjoy – that bright shining star – can help you to focus on what might be right for you. You might not be able to figure out right now how this thing you enjoy will be able to benefit others. You might just enjoy doing it. I think that's fine. I mean, sure, fulfil your obligations to others too – make sure your children are fed and clothed, and attend your work during work hours. But also, make time to play, to experience joy, to experience fun. You and God can figure out together how this new skill will benefit others later.

✎ Write a paragraph, draw a picture or create a collage or mood board that describes your perfect holiday. What would you do just for fun?

Write a paragraph, draw a picture or create a collage or mood board that describes your perfect work day.

RHYTHMS

"Walk with me and work with me — watch how I do it.
Learn the unforced rhythms of grace."
– Jesus (Matthew 11:29 (MSG))

"Happiness is not a matter of intensity but of balance, order,
rhythm and harmony."
– Thomas Merton

What we're aiming for over the course of a year is that most days are pleasantly full with a nice number of tasks, a good amount of space in between appointments, and our priorities neatly taken care of. Then we want some days that are quieter, filled with lazy joy – holidays. These days are spent sitting and reading in front of the fire in winter, or out walking along the beach in summer. Or biking or doing crafts, or solving jigsaw puzzles; whatever doesn't feel like work to you. And finally, some times in the year are busier. In these 'push times' we will have days that are full, maybe even overfull. These are days when we're preparing for a special occasion, or when work gets super heavy as a project nears a deadline.

My husband, Moz, and I have discovered that we, as a couple, work very well when we have a weekend away each quarter. And a day off each week. These are times when we stop to think, to muse, to check in on our regular pace of life and see whether anything needs changing. In between those times, life can get busy, there will be times where we push ourselves and make things happen. But if we stick to having regular breaks we will resist getting caught up in the busy-ness and rush. It is less likely that the overwhelm and struggle will be our regular way of life.

This is a good rhythm for us. I strongly recommend you find one for yourself

Take a look at your calendar. Right now, find a weekend in the next three months that you can designate a 'holiday weekend'. You don't need to go away (though I suggest you do), but choose not to put any activities, meetings, church or family commitments in that weekend. Book it, so that when anyone asks, you can say you are busy.

Take that time to assess your pace of life. Do you need to speed up? Slow down? Are you a victim of busy-creep? Write your thoughts here.

PART 2

HOW

THE EVERYTHING LIST

"Your mind is for having ideas, not holding them."
– David Allen

"Before you eat the elephant, make sure you know what parts you want to eat."
– Todd Stocker

There's a tool that I use for overwhelm that works every time. It is not just recommended by me, a lot of time-management experts use this tool. It's a starting place. It's guaranteed to cut down the clutter in your head and to help you get started, even if you are completely freaking out.

It's called the Everything List.

☑ To use the Everything List, write down everything that you have to do on the piece of paper. Transfer everything on your mental list to the paper list.

No task is too big or too small. Just write it all down.

Things to take off the list

First, are there things on your list that are purely shoulds? Are there items that don't fit with your values? Are there tasks that are obviously not right for your personality? As you look down the list, can you see items that you can easily cross off now that you know more about where you're heading and what your goals are? Are there items that just don't fit?

☑ Go ahead and cross those things off.

See? You've simplified your life already. Well done.

The Everything List

Urgent and important quadrants

Are the tasks on your list urgent and important (quadrant A)? Important but not urgent (quadrant B)? Not important but urgent (quadrant C)? Or neither important nor urgent (quadrant D)?

✎ Divide your tasks among the quadrants on page 57.

Once the tasks are sorted into the quadrants then you have four methods of dealing with them:

- The A tasks are items you really need to attend to now. They can be put onto daily lists over the next week or they can be scheduled in your calendar.

- The B tasks need to be planned for in the future. However, if you don't make the time to do them, they just won't get done. That important thing that you feel called to do will never happen. While there is no urgency, the B tasks are as important as the A tasks. Plan for the B tasks, and put aside time each day or each week to do them. Even though they may be important only to you, they are important.

- The C tasks, the urgent but not so important tasks, can be delegated to someone else. Yes, they need to be done, but they don't necessarily need to be done by you. You have things that only you can do, these tasks can be done by someone else. You might know the perfect person to do them, the person for whom they will be life-giving tasks that they will really enjoy. You might know a teenager who would really enjoy earning a bit of extra cash doing them. You might be in a position to delegate the task to an employee or to a member of your team. Either way, get them off your plate.

- And the final quadrant? The not urgent, not important things? Those things should be dropped. You shouldn't be wasting your time even thinking about them. They are not important, they are not urgent, they do not need to be done. They are weeds clogging up your time garden. Pull them out and throw them away.

IMPORTANT

NOT IMPORTANT

URGENT

NOT URGENT

TIME BUDGET

Parkinson's Law:
Work expands so as to fill the time available for its completion.

Hofstadter's Law:
It always takes longer than you expect, even when you take into account Hofstadter's Law.

We can't do it all. There are just too many possibilities in life. Somehow we need to drop some things. And as you are the only one living your specific life with your specific burdens and challenges and your specific energy levels, you are the one who needs to make the decisions about what your life holds.

The good news is that you've already taken some steps to help you put the important things into your life. This chapter is about making a time budget and the first step in any budget (time or money) is to track what you're already doing. You've already done that. Step one is complete!

Refer to your time tracker, or track another week of your time.

☑ Compare your tracked time to the important–urgent quadrant that you made from your Everything List. How many of the activities from your tracked week belong in quadrants A (important and urgent) or B (important but not urgent)? Are you spending all your time in quadrants C and D? What can you delegate or cut out completely so that you have more time to do the things that are important to you?

_____

_____

_____

_____

☑ Use the knowledge of your time use to inform a time budget. What activities do you need to limit? What are your chosen limits for these activities?

_____

_____

_____

_____

_____

☑ What activities do you need to budget time for? How much time each week or month will you give each of these activites?

_____

_____

_____

_____

_____

_____

Schedule time on your calendar for the important tasks in your time budget, and write your implementation intentions:

☑ I will [behaviour] at [time] in [location]

_____

_____

_____

_____

_____

_____

_____

_____

REST

"Come to me, all you who are weary and burdened, and I will give you rest."
– Jesus (Matthew 11:28, NIV)

"When you rest, you catch your breath and it holds you up, like water wings …"
– Anne Lamott

Rest includes times of silence and solitude, a sabbath (one day off a week), holidays, and, of course, sleep. This may all sound a little idealistic to you, but I encourage you to look out for times when you can take a break, to prioritise sleep, and to entrust your work to God, knowing that he can look after it while you rest.

Open up your calendar and book in two weeks of holidays sometime in the next 12 months. Contact your human resources department or talk to your spouse or book a flight or ask a friend if you can use their beach house. Make it a real commitment. A holiday to look forward to.

✎ Write the dates of your holiday here:

📖 Read some good books about rest and spiritual practices. I suggest:

• *Margin, Restoring Emotional Physical Financial and Time Reserves to Overloaded Lives*
  – Richard Swenson

• *Rest: Why You Get More Done When You Work Less*
  – Alex Soojung-Kim Pang

• *Invitation to Solitude and Silence*
  – Ruth Haley Barton

• *Spacemaker: How to Unplug, Unwind & Think Clearly in the Digital Age*
  – Daniel Sih

DAY-TO-DAY STRATEGIES

"A schedule defends from chaos and whim. It is a net for catching days. It is a scaffolding on which a worker can stand and labor with both hands at sections of time."
– Annie Dillard

Decluttering Question #1:
If I needed this item, where would I look for it first? Take it there now.

Decluttering Question #2:
If I needed this item, would it ever occur to me that I already had one?
– Dana K. White

If I want to fulfil my purpose, have time to follow my dream, and use my unique gifting to serve others, I don't want to waste my time each day looking for my keys, or taking that third trip to the store for the things I didn't remember to buy the other two times. And I definitely don't want to forget my creative ideas or solutions to problems.

Aim to have a limited number of places where you keep things that you need to remember, so that you can find the thing or the memory when it is appropriate to do so, but don't have to keep it in your mind through all the inappropriate times. I call these places 'brain buckets'. I limit the number of buckets that I keep things in, so that I limit the amount of time spent searching for those things and can focus on the activities that are most important to me.

What are three 'next actions' that you can take to increase the organisation in your house? How can you decrease the number of 'brain buckets' that you have? Is there some decluttering you could do to decrease the number of things you need to remember?

1.

2.

3.

REWARDS

*"Work is not man's punishment. It is his reward and his strength
and his pleasure."*
– George Sand

*"Chocolate is the first luxury. It has so many things wrapped up in it:
deliciousness in the moment, childhood memories, and that grin-inducing
feeling of getting a reward for being good."*
– Mariska Hargitay

You might know that there is something that you love to do, you might know it's something God wants you to do, and yet, it's difficult to actually get down and do the thing, and you find yourself putting it off.

If you're having trouble motivating yourself, then maybe you need to have someone else to be accountable to. Someone you can report back to. Someone who will kindly and gently hold a mirror up to you so that you can see whether you're meeting your goals or not. Choose this person carefully. They need to be truthful with you, but also kind.

✎ Write the names of three possible accountability buddies. Then, ask these people whether they will help you in this area. You'll need to explain exactly what you mean, so make a time to meet them for coffee and a chat. We're hoping that one of them will say yes.

1.

2.

3.

✎ Write three goals that you will try to achieve in the next four weeks. Tick them off each week as you achieve them. Were they too easy? Too hard? Or just right?

1.

2.

3.

REVIEW

"Success is not final, failure is not fatal: it is the courage to continue that counts."
– Winston Churchill

"You are never too old to set another goal or to dream a new dream."
– C.S. Lewis

✎ Review the different areas of your life:

Relationships

_____

_____

_____

Serving opportunities/work

_____

_____

_____

Significant projects

_____

_____

_____

Self-care, health and wellness

_____

_____

_____

Money

_____

_____

_____

A new thing

_____

_____

✎ What are your three five-year plans?

1. If things go according to plan, in five years I will …

2. If things take a sharp turn, in five years I will …

3. If time and money were no object and there was no way I could fail, in five years I would …

FAREWELL

It is time to put down this book and to walk into your future, to take steps along the path in front of you, to start doing the good works that God planned in advance for you to do. As you do, I hope that at least some of what I've passed on in this book will be helpful to you. I hope that you're living in shalom, that you're running the race set out for you, that you are feeling God's blessing on your life. I hope that you're starting to say no to things that don't fit you and that you're rejoicing more in saying yes to the things that are really yours to do, that fit your unique gifts, skills and personality.

But I hope most of all that you know that whatever you do, you are valuable as you are. You are precious. God loves you with an amazing unconditional love, just the way you are, right now.

May you work joyfully in the season you are in, may you live peacefully through the different rhythms of life, may you step boldly into success that suits you, and may you grow ever closer to God who created you to be the unique and delightful being that you are.

Join my newsletter at **ruthamos.com.au** to stay connected, to receive links to my blog and podcast, and to find out about my online course. You can support me at **patreon.com/QuietLife** for as little as $1 a month.

Please email me at **ruth@ruthamos.com.au** if you would like me to come and speak at your church or organisation.

Milton Keynes UK
Ingram Content Group UK Ltd.
UKHW022326200324
439690UK00005B/79